"Sometimes I'm afraid of the big bad wolf but then I ask for a hug and I feel better."
Sophia – age 3

"Book therapy for kids! What a great idea! In this fun, beautifully illustrated book filled with great rhymes, Colleen has managed to give phenomenal lessons and actually turn it into a fun, mini therapy session for kids. What a great way to send them off to sleep or enjoy a cozy cuddle together."

    Dr. Eliane Costa Lima, Physician, Professor

"Teachers! Educators! Parents! PLEASE take a look at this book!!! It's a great start to leadership for every little human."

    Mick Petersen, International Bestselling Author, *Stella and the Timekeepers*, *Unwavering Strength* and *Destinies*

"Kids don't get taught in school how to deal with something that should be very basic – their own feelings. The *Feeling Friends* help children, parents and teachers express and embrace their feelings. We need to feel them in order to learn from them. Great educational tool."

    Banafsheh Akhlaghi, Esq., International BestSelling Author of *Beautiful Reminders ~ Anew*.

"OMG – You are amazing! I love this book. We read it as a class and the kids loved it. They were able to talk about the signs of nervousness on her face, in her words, by her actions, etc... they also talked about other feelings and came up with sad, frustrated, calm, silly, mad, shy and bored. I'm thinking about a follow-up activity that deals with the many different ways we can be brave and believe in ourselves. So cool!"

    Denise Oakie, Kindergarten Teacher, HCDSB

Published by Hasmark Publishing
http://www.hasmarkpublishing.com

Copyright© 2017 by Colleen Aynn
First Edition, 2017

No part of this book may be reproduced or transmitted in any form or by any means, electronic or mechanical, including photocopying, recording or by any information storage and retrieval system, without written permission from the author, except for the inclusion of brief quotations in a review.

Disclaimer

This book is designed to provide entertainment to readers and is sold purely for entertainment purposes. This is a work of fiction. Characters, names, places, events, incidents and circumstances are a product of the author's imagination and are used fictitiously. Any resemblance to actual persons, living or dead, business establishments, companies or locales is entirely coincidental and is not intended by the author.

The publisher does not have control over and does not assume responsibility for the author or third party websites. Neither the publisher nor the individual author(s) shall be liable for any physical, psychological, emotional, financial, or commercial damages, including, but not limited to special, incidental, consequential, or other damages.

Permission should be addressed in writing to Colleen Aynn at feelingfriendsfeedback@gmail.com

Illustrator: MATRIX MEDIA SOLUTIONS (P) Ltd.
www.matrixnmedia.com

Cover Designer: Colleen Aynn

Layout: Anne Karklins
annekarklins@gmail.com

ISBN-13: 978-1-988071-62-6
ISBN-10: 1988071623

NERVOUS NELLY

by
Colleen Aynn

Introduction

It's natural to feel nervous, especially when we're doing something new, something we've never done before, that stretches us past our limits and makes us reach for new heights.

The fact that we're nervous means that we care, and that's a good thing, but letting fear come in and steal our dreams isn't the game we want to play.

We can we can let our nerves strangle us and spin us out of control or we can use them as jet fuel to take us where we want to go.

The key is in acknowledging how we're feeling and then transforming those feelings into something useful that can help us.

Fear vs Faith… two opposite ways to view the same situation, and they both require us to believe in something invisible.

Faith = belief something good can happen

Fear = belief something bad can happen

"I've got this."   "It'll never work out."

"But what if I'm wrong?"   "What if I'm right?"

"What if I fail?"   "What if I fly?"

It takes just as much belief either way. So why do we spend so much time worrying???

I used to spend many waking hours nervous. Worrying. I often felt sick to my stomach thinking about future events.

But if we want to play among the stars we've got to BELIEVE!!!

Cultivating faith & nurturing belief is essential to overcoming fear.

Acknowledge the nerves that show up on your doorstep. Sit with the fear. And let it fuel your dreams.

I was tired of living with a pit in my stomach waiting for something bad to happen. So I made a decision;

Fear was allowed in my car, it just wasn't allowed to drive.

It required some focus. And repetition. A LOT of repetition. And I noticed that letting worry go, made room for faith to grow.

So today my friend, I guess I'm saying, "have Faith."

Faith in your dreams.
Faith in yourself.
Faith in the direction you want to go.
Faith in your future.
Faith in love.

You got this,

C xo

For my Mom and all Moms out there who are 'loving worriers'.

I believe in you.

C xo

She was nervous to play, she was nervous to rhyme.
She was nervous whenever she wasn't on time.

She was nervous each time she broke a new rule, and she woke up nervous each day before school.

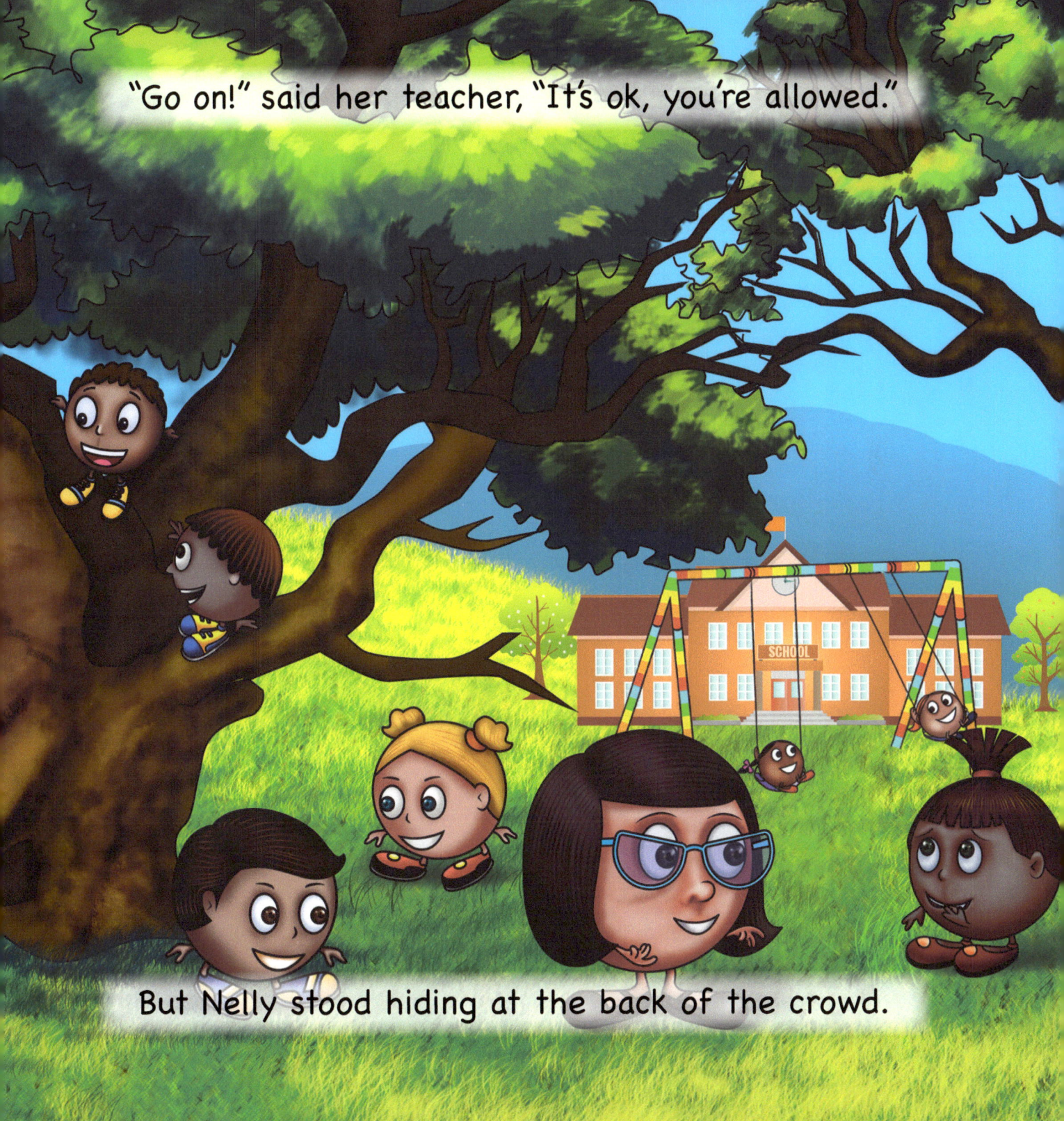

"Go on!" said her teacher, "It's ok, you're allowed."

But Nelly stood hiding at the back of the crowd.

When school was over, Nelly quickly ran home.
She needed to sit in her bedroom, alone.

She turned off the lights and hid under the sheet, when she suddenly felt something tickling her feet.

She peeked out her eyes and started to stare.
A magical unicorn was standing right there!

"Don't spend your time thinking of ways you could lose.
See yourself climbing steady, with wings on your shoes.

Believe you can do it! And see yourself there.
Feel the sun on your face, the wind in your hair."

Nelly closed her eyes and pictured success.
When she opened them, she wouldn't settle for less.

She took one step forward. Then another. Real slow. "Alright, I can do this... ok... here I GOOOOOOOO!"

Nelly climbed as fast as her small feet could fly. She went up, up, UP! Straight into the sky!

As she sat at the top she giggled with glee.
She could see the whole town from atop that big tree.

"If I put my foot here, I can swing my hand 'round. There! Now I've got it!" And she slid to the ground.

"See?" said the unicorn, "You are more than you know. Just trust, relax and step into the flow."

Nelly climbed, wiggled, twisted, enjoying life's curves.
Never more giving in every time she felt nerves.

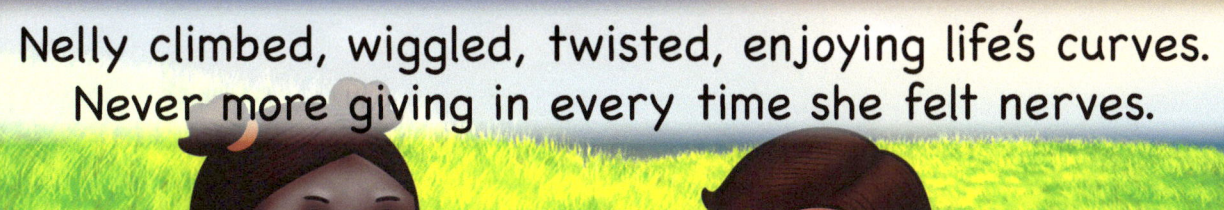

"When I start to feel nervous, I just close my eyes.
I know I can do it, with my eyes on the prize."

About the Author

Colleen is the #1 International Bestselling Author of *Sad Sally*, the first of the *Feeling Friends*. Having experienced firsthand the healing power of expression, she designed the *Feeling Friends* series to empower children and adults to deal with and express their emotions in positive, healthy ways.

Colleen is also a Professional Speaker Coach & Creator of The EPIC System. For over 30 years she spent her life on stages around the globe as a Professional Actress, Singer and Director. Colleen has now taken this knowledge and experience and broken it down into easy, implementable steps, inspiring people to boldly express themselves and bring their unique voices to the world. Her interactive workshops and online courses teach others how to communicate their message with influence and confidence both on stage and in front of the camera. Come on over to colleenaynn.com and say hi!

Colleen still loves to get up on stage and belt out a tune, and these days she's most often joined by her awesome husband, Bruno and little firecracker, Emilia. Colleen lives in Burlington, Ontario.

The Literary Fairies

we make your literary wish come true

"Feeling Friends"

are excited to introduce you to their new friends

The Literary Fairies

TLF is a cool place where you can find out
how YOU could become a published author or
how to help grant a literary wish.
Have an adult visit TLF website for more details about
what we do and how you can help, and also get your
FREE colouring pages and "fill-in-the-blank story"

http://theliteraryfairies.com/free-for-kids/

Join *Sad Sally, Mad Michael, Nervous Nelly* and *Happy Hannah* and all their friends as they navigate through big, emotional days with the help of some wise animal friends.

Feeling Friends help parents and kids alike, deal with and express their feelings in constructive, healthy ways.

For more tools, tips and tricks or to order this magnificent series visit
feelingfriendsbooks.com
for your BONUS gifts today!

Sad Sally

Happy Hannah

Nervous Nelly

Mad Michael

www.ingramcontent.com/pod-product-compliance
Lightning Source LLC
Chambersburg PA
CBHW041537040426
42446CB00002B/128